Yosemite
National Park

John Hamilton

VISIT US AT
WWW.ABDOPUB.COM

Published by ABDO Publishing Company, 4940 Viking Drive, Suite 622, Edina, Minnesota 55435.
Copyright ©2005 by Abdo Consulting Group, Inc. International copyrights reserved in all countries.
No part of this book may be reproduced in any form without written permission from the publisher.
ABDO & Daughters™ is a trademark and logo of ABDO Publishing Company.

Printed in the United States.

Editor: Paul Joseph
Graphic Design: John Hamilton
All photos and illustrations by John Hamilton, except Library of Congress, p. 12 (Theodore Roosevelt
with John Muir), National Park Service, p. 13 (map of Yosemite), Sierra Club, p. 18 (Hetch Hetchy
Valley).

Library of Congress Cataloging-in-Publication Data

Hamilton, John, 1959–
    Yosemite National Park / John Hamilton.
       p. cm. — (National parks)
    Summary: Discusses the history of this national park, its geological features, plant and animal life,
dangers in the park, and efforts to preserve it.
    Includes bibliographical references and index.
    ISBN 1-59197-428-3
    1. Yosemite National Park (Calif.)—Juvenile literature. [1. Yosemite National Park (Calif.)
2. National parks and reserves.] I. Title. II. National parks (ABDO Publishing Company)

    F868.Y6H195 2005
    917.94'47—dc21

                            2003045397

Contents

*Water cascades down
Lower Yosemite Fall.*

Half Dome towers over Yosemite Valley.

The Yosemite Adventure

Yosemite National Park is one of the "crown jewel" parks of the United States, beloved by millions of people. Located in east-central California, it is less than a day's drive from huge population centers, including Los Angeles and San Francisco. But the rest of the country flocks to Yosemite as well, and for good reason. There are few places on Earth with scenery as breathtaking as Yosemite, with panoramas embracing mountain peaks and deep valleys straddled by soaring cliffs of granite. Where else can you find high waterfalls, peaceful meadows, and forest groves filled with giant sequoias, the world's biggest living things, all in one park?

Yosemite sits in a mountain range called the Sierra Nevada, also known simply as the Sierras. *Sierra* is a Spanish word that means saw, and *nevada* means snowy. From a distance, the mountains look like the snow-capped peaks of a giant, overturned saw. Yosemite, roughly the size of Rhode Island at 1,200 square miles (3,108 square km), sits perched directly within this mountain landscape.

Preserved as a national park in 1890, Yosemite gives us a glimpse of raw nature, wilderness as it once was. This is especially true for people who get off the roads and put on their hiking boots. More than 800 miles (1,287 km) of marked trails crisscross the park.

Backpackers set out on an early-morning hike at Tuolumne Meadows, in Yosemite's High Country.

Most of Yosemite is untamed backcountry, with enough solitude and wide-open spaces to satisfy even the most restless soul. But it is Yosemite Valley for which the park is most well known. There are only four main roads that lead into the park, one for each point of the compass, and they all lead into the valley.

On a warm summer's day, there might be close to 14,000 people crowded into this mile-wide, seven-mile-long glacier-carved canyon. They've come to see the open meadows, waterfalls, and towering cliffs that make the valley famous. Legendary names like El Capitan, Half Dome, and Bridalveil Fall loom overhead. Underfoot lie still meadows, punctuated with the color of wildflowers and oak groves. The Merced River winds gracefully through the scenery. At dusk, the cliffs high above are set ablaze in a riot of color. On other days, clouds and mist descend and wrap the valley in a hush, muting the landscape in an almost mystical way. There are no dull days in Yosemite.

In a typical year, more than 3.5 million people will visit Yosemite. About 90 percent of them will go to the valley, which occupies only about one percent of the entire park. But Yosemite is so much more, from the historic centers at Wawona, to the hundreds of giant sequoia trees in Mariposa Grove, to the alpine thrill of exploring the Tioga Road and Tuolumne Meadows.

With an elevation range from 2,000 feet (610 m) to 13,123 feet (4,000 m), Yosemite National Park supports several distinct vegetation zones, from oak woodlands all the way up to alpine. Because of this, many kinds of animals are found here, including deer, chipmunks, bats, black bear, marmots, and mountain lions. More than 150 species of birds make their home in Yosemite, including great gray owls. Plant life is also abundant here, ranging from dogwood, red fir, dwarf willow, and of course the giant sequoia. There are more than 160 rare plant species nestled on the grounds of this diverse landscape.

Indian paintbrushes bloom on a trail near Tenaya Lake.

More than 3.5 million people visit Yosemite National Park each year. The most popular destination in the park by far is Yosemite Valley (above). The Ahwahneechee Indians called Bridalveil Fall (below) "Spirit of the Puffing Wind."

8 "No temple made with hands can compare with Yosemite." —John Muir

Formed by Fire and Ice

The history of Yosemite National Park began 500 million years ago, when the region lay beneath a shallow sea on the western edge of North America. Sedimentary rock formed on the seabed, the result of eons of silt, mud, and marine creature deposits. The area was then lifted up above sea level, eventually becoming a mountain range surrounded by a chain of volcanoes. It resembled the Cascade Range of mountains that we see today in the Pacific Northwest.

Molten rock at the roots of the volcanoes formed into granite, one of the hardest rocks on Earth. Over millions of years, most of the upper layers of softer sedimentary and volcanic rocks weathered and eroded away, leaving behind the core granite mountains.

Ten million years ago the Sierra Nevada area tilted and uplifted. Streams and rivers became steeper. After millions of years, deep canyons formed. Then, starting about 1 million years ago, a series of ice ages filled the canyons with glaciers. Some of the glaciers may have been as thick as 4,000 feet (1,219 m), engulfing many of the area's mountain peaks. These rivers of ice moved downward and scoured the landscape, polishing the granite and creating the U-shaped valleys, waterfalls, and lakes that we see today.

"Every rock in its walls seems to glow with life."
John Muir

The steep, granite walls of Yosemite Valley (above) were formed by magma rising to the surface millions of years ago. Erosion from rivers and glaciers cut the deep U-shaped valleys found in the park today. When the glaciers retreated, they left behind a series of waterfalls and lakes. Tenaya Lake (below) was gouged out by the Tuolumne Glacier.

History

Native Americans lived in the Yosemite area as long as 8,000 years ago. By the mid 1800's the Indians were mainly Southern Miwok, or as they called themselves, the Ahwahneechee.

The Miwok had a rich cultural heritage that embraced religion, politics, and song. They made use of the ecosystem and changed it to suit their needs. The grasslands and oak groves of today's Yosemite Valley are probably a result of intentional burning of underbrush by the Indians.

After the discovery of gold in the Sierra Nevada foothills in 1848, thousands of fortune-seeking miners conflicted with the Native Americans. The first known exploration by non-Indians of Yosemite Valley happened in 1851 during the Mariposa Indian War. Later that same year, the Miwok people were forced off their land to the Fresno River Reservation.

President Theodore Roosevelt (left) and John Muir at Yosemite.

Word quickly spread of the beauty in Yosemite's valleys and mountains. Writers, artists, and photographers made the area famous, and by 1855 the first tourists were already flocking to Yosemite.

Visitors and development rapidly threatened to disrupt the area's fragile ecosystem. Thanks to the pioneering work of naturalist John Muir and others, President Abraham Lincoln on June 30, 1864, set aside Yosemite Valley and Mariposa Grove of Giant Sequoias to protect them for the enjoyment of all people.

Setting aside and preserving public land was a new idea, one that led to the first official national park, Yellowstone, in 1872. On October 1, 1890, Yosemite itself became a national park.

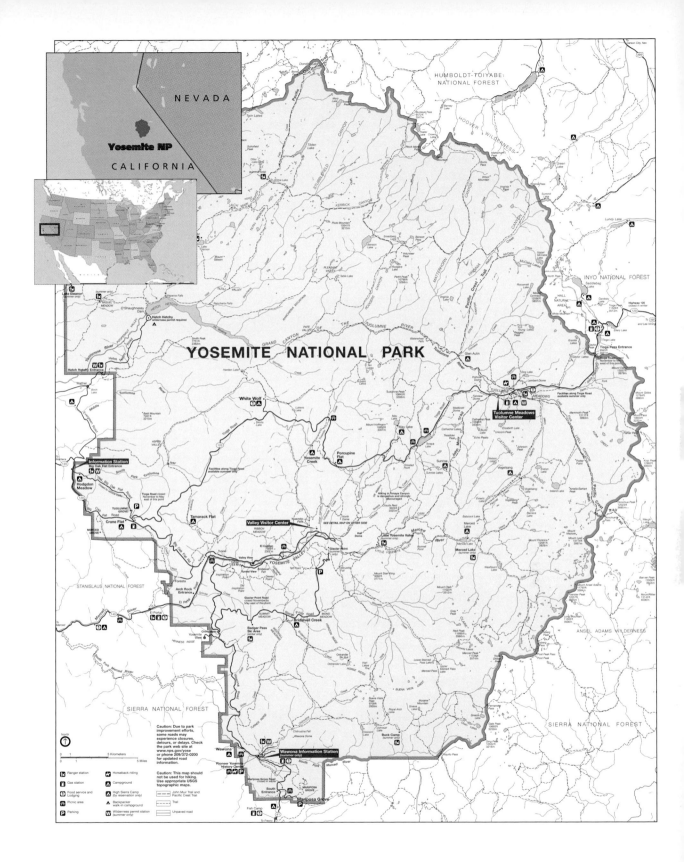

Yosemite Valley

Yosemite Valley is the heart of Yosemite National Park. The valley is world famous for its collection of waterfalls, meadows, towering cliffs, and wildlife, all packed in a cathedral-like expanse measuring only seven square miles (18 square km). While most of the park is closed to cars during winter, the valley is open all year.

After the last ice age, runoff from melting glaciers flooded the valley and created an enormous lake. Eventually, silt and mud filled in the lake, which formed the flat valley floor that we find today. The valley floor sits at an elevation of about 4,000 feet (1,219 m) above sea level, while on either side of the valley cliffs and domes such as El Capitan and Half Dome soar up to 4,000 feet (1,219 m) higher.

A tour of the valley contains many highlights. To properly explore the area takes several days. Still, many people are content to zip around the park loop road in a day and take in as many features as possible. The park experience is different for each person, but the beauty of Yosemite is so extraordinary that it can be a life-changing event no matter how fleeting the visit.

The floor of Yosemite Valley is wide and flat, the result of ice age glaciers.

"A glitter of green and golden wonder in a vast edifice of stone and space."
—Ansel Adams

Hikers get soaked at the base of Bridalveil Fall.

If you enter the valley from the south, you'll pass through Wawona Tunnel. At the tunnel's east end is a parking lot next to Tunnel View Overlook, one of the most stunning vistas on the planet. Laid out beneath is Yosemite Valley, often called "the Incomparable Valley," in all its scenic splendor.

Many major features can be seen from here. El Capitan, a huge granite dome, looms to the north, seemingly guarding the valley entrance. It is the world's largest exposed granite cliff, twice as high as the Rock of Gibraltar. If you look through binoculars, you can often spot rock climbers ascending the 3,593-foot (1,095 m) summit. Scaling the cliff usually takes more than a day. In the evening you can see climbers hanging from slings and bags, where they spend the night until resuming their ascent the next morning.

Opposite El Capitan is Bridalveil Fall, which cascades 620 feet (189 m), sometimes in a late-afternoon display of rainbow-hued mist. Off in the distance, at the end of the valley, sits Half Dome, a glacier-scoured monolith of gray granite.

As one travels up the valley, more features come into view, each as dazzling as the next. Waterfalls seem to appear around every corner: Vernal Fall, Nevada Fall, Illilouette Fall. In the north central part of the valley, near the Valley Visitor Center, is Yosemite Falls. The upper, middle, and lower section together form one of the highest waterfalls in the world, at 2,425 feet (739 m).

El Capitan is the world's largest exposed granite cliff.

Rafters on the Merced River.

Spectacular cliffs and leaping waterfalls are not all that Yosemite Valley has to offer. Meadows, oak woodlands, and forests of pine and cedar trees harbor wildflowers, butterflies, and a multitude of animals and birds. And winding its way through the middle of the valley is the Merced River. Rafters can often be seen floating lazily down its current on warm summer days.

For a stunning view of the east end of the valley, visitors can hike or drive to Glacier Point, a 3,200-foot (975-m) overlook from which you can also spot the peaks of the High Sierra Range to the north. It's a perfect place to witness a Yosemite sunset, when the granite cliffs of Half Dome and other mountains light up in a pastel glow of orange and yellow.

Many visitors don't realize that Yosemite Valley has a twin called Hetch Hetchy Valley, which lies just to the north inside the park. Equally spectacular as Yosemite Valley, much of Hetch Hetchy was submerged underwater when the O'Shaughnessy Dam was completed in 1923. Water from the reservoir is used to provide drinking water and power to the city of San Francisco. The flooding of the valley was a bitter defeat for conservationists such as John Muir. Today, there is talk of removing the dam and restoring the valley to its original state.

Hetch Hetchy Valley before it was partially submerged by the O'Shaughnessy Dam in 1923.

The view from Glacier Point (above and below) is spectacular, with the eastern end of Yosemite Valley laid out 3,200 feet (975 m) below. A favorite with tourists, the National Park Service added a new amphitheater and concession facility to Glacier Point in 1997. Several areas of nearby wilderness were also restored.

Mariposa Grove

If measured by total volume, giant sequoia trees are the largest living things on the planet. Giant sequoias, also called Sierra redwoods, can reach heights of up to 311 feet (95 m). The trunks at their base can reach 40 feet (12 m) in diameter. They weigh up to 2.7 million pounds (1,226 metric tons) each, with bark that measures 31 inches (79 cm) thick. The protective bark is so thick and tough that it totally protects the trees against brush fires and insect invasions.

There are three groves of these enormous trees in Yosemite National Park, including Tuolumne Grove and Merced Grove. But it is Mariposa Grove of Giant Sequoias that is the largest and most famous.

Located in the southern part of the park, Mariposa Grove holds approximately 500 mature sequoia trees. Some of them are extremely old. The most famous tree in the grove is Grizzly Giant, which scientists estimate is more than 2,700 years old, making it Yosemite's oldest living sequoia.

Visitors come from all over the world to marvel at the giant sequoia trees, some of which can reach 40 feet (95 m) in diameter at their base.

Giant Sequoias can live for thousands of years.

Grizzly Giant is one of the world's largest trees.

A young visitor stands next to the roots of a fallen Sequoia tree.

Sequoia trees need mild, wet winters and dry, warm summers to thrive. They also need fire. Well-meaning forestry officials in times past put out or suppressed any fire that started in the park. We now know that fire is vital for sequoias to reproduce. Fire dries out the trees' seed cones, which then causes them to pop and collectively release millions of oat flake-sized seeds to the ground below.

Unfortunately, in addition to causing fewer seed releases, fire suppression has also resulted in too much undergrowth on the ground. Sequoia seeds need to land on bare mineral soil for them to germinate and take root. In recent years, prescribed fires by the National Park Service have been set to simulate natural fires. Hopefully this will improve the health of the forest and restore it to a more natural and productive state.

Mariposa Grove and its majestic trees can be visited any time of year, even in winter for those who cross-country ski. During the summer months guided tram tours highlight the main features of the area. For the best views, however, take a hike along one of the trails that meander among these stately giants.

Just down the road from Mariposa Grove is the Wawona area, home to Native Americans for thousands of years. In 1875, a hotel was built for the budding tourist industry. The historic Wawona Hotel is still in use today. A short walk away, after crossing a covered bridge, is the Pioneer Yosemite History Center, which displays historic buildings and a horse stable. You can ride on a horse-drawn carriage to get a small taste of what it was like over a century ago for adventurous park visitors.

A horse-drawn carriage races through the Pioneer Yosemite History Center.

The High Country

North of Yosemite Valley is a huge area of the park that is more remote, more wild. This land is often called the High Country, a rugged mountain wilderness of snowy peaks and deep, glacier-cut canyons. Scattered within this Sierra Nevada alpine scenery are still meadows and crystal-clear mountain lakes. Sturdy hikers and campers come here to escape the summer tourists that crowd the Yosemite Valley and Mariposa Grove areas. There are hundreds of miles of marked trails that wander deep into Yosemite's interior, challenging even the most experienced backpackers. But Yosemite's High Country offers something for everyone. Even beginners or casual nature-lovers can find this rugged area very rewarding.

Unicorn Peak in the Cathedral Range can be seen in the distance from Tuolumne Meadows.

The Tuolumne River flows through Yosemite's High Country.

The scenic Tioga Road crosses the High Country, running approximately 50 miles (80 km) through the middle of the park. The road begins about nine miles (14 km) north of Yosemite Valley, at a place called Crane Flat. Already you are at 6,200 feet (1,890 m) in elevation. Tioga Road was originally an old mining path, but has since been modernized to make the twists and turns less hazardous. Even so, driving parts of the road, which is open only during the summer months, can be a breathtaking experience.

From Crane Flat the road snakes eastward across the alpine landscape, with frequent stopping places to hike or simply view the many lakes, meadows, and majestic granite peaks and domes towering overhead. The road climbs steadily until it reaches Tioga Pass. At 9,945 feet (3,031 m), it is the highest automobile pass in the state of California.

Tuolumne Meadows is a favorite destination for people exploring the High Country. Located about 55 miles (89 km) from Yosemite Valley on the Tioga Road, it is the largest subalpine meadow in the Sierra Nevada Range, resting at 8,600 feet (2,621 m) in elevation. In the spring and summer, wildflowers paint the meadow in spectacular colors. Wildlife thrives around every corner, and the Tuolumne River begins its descent toward the western edge of the park. A visitor center and campground make Tuolumne Meadows a natural place to begin overnight backpacking trips into the park's rugged interior.

A backpacker sets off on a Yosemite High Country hiking trip.

Olmsted Point (above) is a steep slope of cracked granite strewn with scattered glacial erratics and sturdy cypress trees that grow right out of the rock. Glacial erratics are large boulders that are carried by glaciers and left when the ice melts away. Frost on meadow vegetation (below) shows how cold it can get in the higher elevations even in summer.

Future Challenges

Yosemite National Park is such a spectacular piece of landscape that it is a favorite among Americans, who visit the park by the millions each year. But some say Yosemite is being loved to death. Overcrowding, especially in the relatively small space of Yosemite Valley, has become a serious problem in recent decades. There are simply too many tourists who wish to visit the park all at the same time, especially in the warm summer months when most people take their vacations.

To decrease traffic jams and pollution, Yosemite began running shuttle busses in the early 1970s. Visitors are encouraged to walk rather than drive. This has helped somewhat, but overcrowding remains one of the chief complaints among park visitors.

In the late 1990s, restoration projects along the Merced River were started after a series of rock slides and floods in the valley. Park managers are attempting to let nature reshape the park, the way it has for millions of years. Black oak woodlands and meadows are being restored to how they were before being trampled by crowds of people.

Some species of wildlife are also being reintroduced into the park, after a long absence due to hunting or habitat destruction. These include bighorn sheep and peregrine falcons.

Many volunteers and private organizations, including the Sierra Club and the Yosemite Fund, have teamed up with the National Park Service to restore and preserve this magnificent park, preserving it for future generations.

Half Dome reflected in the Merced River. *"The real voyage of discovery consists not in seeking new landscapes but in having new eyes."*—Marcel Proust

Glossary

ALPINE

In high mountains, alpine is the vegetation zone above the timberline, where it is too cold for trees to grow.

ECOSYSTEM

A biological community of animals, plants, and bacteria, all of whom live together in the same physical or chemical environment.

FEDERAL LANDS

Much of America's land, especially in the western part of the country, is maintained by the United States federal government. These are public lands owned by all U.S. citizens. There are many kinds of federal lands. National parks, like Yosemite, are federal lands that are set aside so that they can be preserved. Other federal lands, such as national forests or national grasslands, are used in many different ways, including logging, ranching, and mining. Much of the land surrounding Yosemite is maintained by the government, including several national forests and wildlife refuges.

FOREST SERVICE

The United States Department of Agriculture (USDA) Forest Service was started in 1905 to manage public lands in national forests and grasslands. The Forest Service today oversees an area of 191 million acres (77.3 million hectares), which is an amount of land about the same size as Texas. In addition to protecting and managing America's public lands, the Forest Service also conducts forestry research and helps many state government and private forestry programs.

GLACIER

A glacier is often called a river of ice. It is made of thick sheets of ice and snow. Glaciers slowly move downhill, scouring and smoothing the landscape.

GRANITE

A very hard, course igneous rock created by volcanic action. Granite can range from gray to pink, and is composed mainly of feldspar, quartz, mica, and hornblende. Most of the rock formations found in Yosemite National Park are made of granite.

MONOLITH

A monolith is a large, single block of stone. Yosemite has many huge monoliths, such as El Capitan or Half Dome.

SUBALPINE

A growth zone in the mountains that exists just below the timberline.

A golden summer sunset lights up the cliffs along Yosemite Valley.

Index

DATE DUE

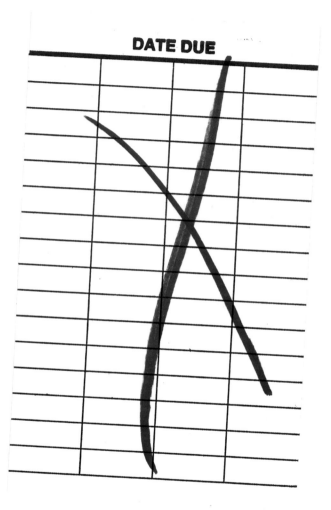